Anna Lia &
The Magical Christmas Gifts

For Amelia and Anneleise
Never stop believing

ISBN: 978-0-9952444-1-2

Copyright Donna Pidlubny 2016
Published by Home Free
Toronto, Ontario, Canada

When Anna Lia was quite small she sensed magic in everything. In the songs of the birds, that woke her each morning. In the beautiful flowers, that opened their petals to embrace the warm morning sun. In how the bees found the nectar, then turned it into the best sweet treat ever. Even in how the thick grass next to the cooked fence grew taller each day, as if it was trying to reach the sun.

Everything was perfect she thought,
. . . everything was just as it should be.

Anna Lia loved to get up early to say good morning to the sun. She sang with the birds and danced on the damp morning grass. She would twirl till her dress looked like the petals of a flower. When she lost her balance and fell down on the soft grass, Anna Lia would stare up at the cloud animals and watch them float by.

Life was truly magical.

The tall grass next to the crooked fence was a wonderful place to play. The grass grew so tall and strong that it looked like trees in a miniature magical forest.

Sometimes Anna Lia thought she saw Tiny people in her magical forest, but she couldn't be sure. Mr. Young, the funny old man from across the street, told her she had to believe it before she could see it.

And Anna Lia believed with all her heart.

One day Anna Lia decided she would make a small house in the tall grass forest. Perhaps the Tiny people would come and visit, or even make it their home. Maybe, just maybe, she would finally see one.

She got to work with her craft scissors, clearing an area that was just the right size. Bending and weaving the tall grass she shaped walls and a roof. To make it more inviting and comfortable, she placed soft grass clippings on the floor.

Early the next morning, Anna Lia awoke from a dream about a tiny person sleeping in the grass house. Wanting to see if the dream was real, she jumped out of bed and quietly went to the back door.

With the sun just showing its crown, she tiptoed outside to the tall grass forest, next to the crooked fence. As the first morning light was beginning to inch its way into the small house she thought she saw something. She blinked her eyes to try and make her vision clearer.

At first, she didn't know what she was seeing. When she realized what it was, Anna Lia squealed with delight. There in front of her, a Tiny person was sleeping on the bed of soft grass.

She held her hand over her mouth to try and muffle the sound of her excitement. As hard as she tried to be quiet, the Tiny person woke up and ran away so fast he forgot to take his tiny shoes. Anna Lia giggled with delight.

It was true, they do exist. She had seen him with her very own eyes.

Anna Lia got an idea. She ran to her room to get some doll house furniture. On a small tray, she put a dolls bed, table, chair, and some dishes. They would be just the right size for the Tiny person to use.

Quietly she went to the kitchen and put some cereal on the plate. Just one "O" was enough for such a Tiny person. She also put a drop of water in the teeny cup for her guest.

Pleased with herself she carefully carried everything to the tall grass forest next to the crooked fence. Anna Lia arranged the furniture, put the breakfast on the table and the tiny shoes next to the bed. She was very pleased with herself and thought everything was perfect.

She sat back on her heels and waited,
 . . . and waited,
  . . . but nothing happened.

All this excitement was very hungry work. When the growls in her stomach got really loud, Anna Lia went inside to get her own cereal. She ate as fast as she could then ran back outside to the small house in the tall grass forest next to the crooked fence.

Was he there eating his breakfast? Did he like what she had brought him? If she said hello would he say it back? What would he sound like? She was so excited.

But when she looked inside the small grass house it was empty.

Her disappointment quickly faded when she realized the Tiny person had come back. The shoes, cereal, and water were all gone. She jumped for joy and clapped her hands with excitement.

She could hardly wait to tell her friend, Mr. Young.

Mr. Young, the funny old man from across the street, came every afternoon to work in the garden. Anna Lia loved to help him with digging, planting and watering. He told her stories while they worked. He had some very good stories, and he always listened to hers.

Sometimes they would sit on the side of the garden and rest, eating snow peas or strawberries while they talked and laughed together.

It was one of those times that Anna Lia told him about the Tiny person she had come upon. Mr. Young was very interested in what she had to say and pleased to hear that she offered the Tiny person food. It made him smile, and that made Anna Lia very happy.

As the days grew shorter, the summer plants turned from deep greens to shades of yellow, orange, red, and brown. Anna Lia was sad to see the food she left for the Tiny person was no longer being taken. She worried that something had happened to him.

While in the pumpkin patch, Mr. Young asked her what was wrong. She told him about her concern. He explained that the days were growing shorter and the nights were getting colder, so the Tiny person had probably moved into a warm place for the coming winter.

What a relief. She felt so much better. But she still missed the Tiny person even though she had only seen him that one time.

When the last of the vegetables were out of the garden, Mr. Young didn't come anymore. The tall grass forest turned from green to brown, and the days grew shorter and colder. Anna Lia wondered where the Tiny person had moved to and how he was doing. Mr. Young had told her not to worry and that he would probably return when winter changed back into spring.

But she couldn't help it, she still worried.

One day the ground was covered in white glistening snow. Anna Lia was so excited to go out and play. The snow was sticky and just perfect for rolling into balls. She made three of them, a small, medium and large. Anna Lia stacked them on top of each other and built a snow person next to the crooked fence. She used a bucket for a hat, stones for the eyes and mouth and a pinecone for the nose, and finished it off with a scarf around the neck.

Anna Lia was very proud of what she had created. It was so much fun that she made a tiny matching friend. She put it on the crooked fence next to her bigger snow person. Maybe the Tiny person would see it and smile.

When Anna Lia played inside she pretended that the Tiny person was inside too. She had returned the furniture to her doll house just before the snow arrived. Every day she would put cereal on the plate and water in the cup. She wished the Tiny person had moved into her house to stay warm for the winter, but sadly the food was always there the next day.

One day a Christmas tree was put up in the big living room. It was decorated with lights and ornaments that sparkled. Gifts were wrapped and put under the tree. It was such an exciting time of year, filled with wonderful smells and beautiful music that everyone seemed to know the words to.

Anna Lia had collected several pinecones that summer and she placed one inside her doll house. She wanted it to look like Christmas in there too. Maybe, just maybe the Tiny person would see it and come by for a visit.

Anna Lia loved to help make the Christmas goodies. The wonderful smells of cookies and cakes filled the air as the treats were packed into boxes and tins to give as gifts. This gave Anna Lia an idea.

She cut a small piece of homemade chocolate marshmallow fudge and wrapped it up in a Christmas napkin, and tied it up with a ribbon. Anna Lia put it next to the pinecone Christmas tree in her doll house. She hoped the Tiny person would find it.

Even though she didn't know if the Tiny person had moved into her house for the winter, Anna Lia still believed with all her heart.

The next morning the bundle was gone. In its place was a small bag with a picture of a Christmas tree, the number 24, and a picture of the moon and stars.

Today was the 24th. Tomorrow was Christmas. She thought that maybe the small bag had a Christmas gift inside, so she carefully peeked into the bundle. But it was empty. Maybe the moon and the stars meant that it was for tonight, Christmas Eve.

That night, during the Christmas Eve meal she told her parents her story. They smiled but were very surprised when Anna Lia showed them the little bag.

They were puzzled by the message too. Both her parents looked inside the small bag but didn't see anything either.

Her mother pushed just one finger inside the opening. It was a very small bag after all. Imagine her surprise when she could feel something inside the bag. Then with a big knowing smile, she went to the Christmas tree and sprinkled some of the invisible contents onto the tree. Nothing seemed to happen, so the little bag was put aside as they prepared for guests to arrive.

Later that evening Anna Lia saw something sparkling on the tree that she hadn't noticed before. The tree was covered with candy. Foil wrapped chocolate, candy canes, and many different kinds of treats.

Anna Lia giggled as she gobbled up a treat. She invited everyone to have some, and all enjoyed the magical gift. Anna Lia finally realized the meaning of the mysterious symbols. On Christmas Eve, as the stars come out, sprinkle some of the fine dust on the tree. Before long delicious treats will appear.

Everyone agreed this was truly a magical gift.

Year after year the magic happened. The bag was never empty on Christmas Eve. The treats were different each time but they always appeared a short time after the invisible magical Christmas dust was sprinkled on the tree.

Anna Lia never saw the Tiny person again, but each year, on the day before Christmas Eve, she would leave a small package of homemade goodies for the Tiny person to find.

Sometimes it was chocolate marshmallow fudge, sometimes it was some delicious cake, and sometimes it was cookies baked especially for the Tiny person.

Each Christmas Eve morning her delicious gift would be gone. In the evening when the stars came out, Anna Lia would reach inside the little bag and sprinkle a small amount of the magical Christmas dust on the decorated tree.

The yummy candies would always appear soon after.

When Anna Lia moved into her own home she continued the tradition. She made up little bags just like the one she was given, with just a pinch of the magical dust inside. Anna Lia gave them to friends and family along with the story of how she came to get the gift, even writing it down so everyone could enjoy it.

The magic worked for them too.

When Anna Lia had children and grandchildren of her own, they would ask her about the Christmas dust, and she would tell her story.

Anna Lia knew it probably wasn't the same Tiny person who came to get the goodies each year. Instead, the tradition carried on with his children, and later his grandchildren.

She thought they might ask him similar questions to what she had been asked over the years.

She imagined he would tell the story of the giant child he met in the tall grass forest, next to the crooked fence. How she had made him a shelter to protect him from the summer rain, and gave him food to eat just when he needed it most.

He would say to them:

"And just when winter is at it's darkest, she gives us a wonderful gift. That is truly magical."

Chocolate Marshmallow Fudge *(5 minute fudge)*

1-2/3 cups white sugar

2/3 cup evaporated milk

1/2 teaspoon of salt

1-1/2 cups of chocolate chips

1-1/2 cups of miniature marshmallows
or regular ones that have been cut up

1/2 cup chopped nuts (optional)

1 teaspoon vanilla

Mix milk and sugar in a saucepan over medium heat. Bring to boiling, and cook for 5 minutes, stirring constantly. Remove from heat and add remaining ingredients right away. Keep stirring until all the marshmallows have melted. *If needed keep on very low heat and keep stirring.*

Pour into a 9x9 butter pan or round cake pan. Let cool and cut into squares.

If the fudge doesn't set, it probably means the marshmallows didn't melt completely. You can put the fudge back on low heat, stir and dissolve.